100% Trivia About Money

by Hubert E. Ellis

HOUGHTON MIFFLIN BOSTON

PHOTOGRAPHY CREDITS
Cover © Bureau of Engraving and Printing; **4** © AP/Wide World Photos; **5** © NMPFT/SSPL/The Image Works

Printed in China

ISBN 10: 0-618-89931-6
ISBN 13: 978-0-618-89931-9

9 10 11 12 0940 16 15 14 13
4500432011

Money, Money, Money

The U.S. Treasury Department currently prints six bills called notes or currency. They have values of $1, $5, $10, $20, $50, and $100. The $100 note has been the most valuable note printed since 1969.

The Treasury Department prints money at the Bureau of Engraving and Printing plants in Washington, D.C., and Fort Worth, Texas. Together, those two plants use 18 tons of ink to print new money every single day. They print 37 million notes per day, which is a total value of $696,000,000! About 95% of the new notes replace old notes that are worn out from use. About 45% of the notes printed each day are $1 notes.

Read·Think·Write If $1 is 1% of $100, what percent is $5? $20? $50?

Do you know what the most widely used note is? You might be surprised. It's the $20 note. Here is how long most notes are used before they wear out:

$1	22 months
$5	24 months
$10	18 months
$20	25 months
$50	55 months
$100	60 months

Why do you suppose $10 notes wear out more quickly than others? It's a mystery!

Read·Think·Write $10 is half of $20. What percent of $20 is $10?

Most Valuable Notes

Size and Value

Until 1969, the United States had \$500; \$1,000; \$5,000; and \$10,000 notes. You probably will not find one at a store or a bank. You might see one in a museum.

The notes with the least value ever printed were made during the Civil War. During the war, the metal usually used in coins was needed for other things. The notes, called Fractional Currency, came in 5-cent, 10-cent, 25-cent, and 50-cent notes.

Read·Think·Write What percent of \$1 is 25 cents? What fraction of \$1 is 25 cents?

No matter what its value, U.S. notes are the same size. Today, each note is 2.61 inches wide by 6.14 inches long. Before 1929, U.S. notes were 3.125 inches wide by 7.4218 inches long. How much narrower is a note today? How much shorter is it?

$$\begin{array}{rl} 3.125 & \text{in.} \\ -\ \underline{2.61} & \text{in.} \\ 0.515 & \text{in. narrower} \end{array} \qquad \begin{array}{rl} 7.4218 & \text{in.} \\ -\ \underline{6.14} & \text{in.} \\ 1.2818 & \text{in. shorter} \end{array}$$

Notes are made from 75% cotton. The rest is linen, which is a strong fiber that comes from the flax plant.

Read·Think·Write If 75% of the material used to make a note is cotton and the rest is linen, what percent of the note is linen?

Fractional Currency

New Money and Bad Money

Notes are redesigned every 7 to 10 years to keep ahead of counterfeiters—people who make money that looks like real notes. Here is what you will notice in new notes:

- The portrait is larger and off-center.
- A watermark looks like the portrait.
- There is more color. The $10 note includes background colors of orange, yellow, and red.

- The ink of the number in the lower right corner changes colors when held at different angles.
- Tiny print looks like a thin line to the naked eye.
- Serial numbers appear twice on the new notes.

Notes may be damaged by fire, flood, or other disasters. In 2005, the Bureau of Engraving and Printing handled more than 26,000 claims for damaged notes. The Bureau paid out more than $97,000,000 to replace the notes.

Wet notes can be separated and dried. If they are damaged by more than just water, they can be taken to a bank. The bank may be able to help.

The Bureau of Engraving and Printing handles badly damaged notes. If a note has been damaged, its owner must be able to show at least 51% of the note. If 50% or less of the note remains, the owner needs to prove that the note existed.

When notes wear out, they are shredded so that they can no longer be used.

There is a law against marking or destroying notes so that they can no longer be used. But who would want to destroy money? It's worth money!

Read·Think·Write If you have about 75% of a $10 note that was damaged in a house fire, what can you do?

Responding

Vocabulary

1. Summarize If 95% of the notes printed each day replace old, worn-out notes, what percentage of notes printed each day is new money?
2. What fraction of a dollar is a 5-cent note? What percent of a dollar is it? What fraction of a dollar is a 25-cent note? What percent of a dollar is it?
3. Suppose that you have $100. What percent of that amount does a $10 note represent? What percent of $100 is $60?

Activity

With a partner, discuss and answer these questions:

- What percent of the notes that are printed each day are made from trees?
- Why is the quarter called a quarter?
- Suppose that you found a 25-cent Fractional Currency note. List at least three things you could do with the note. Which one would you do, and why?
- Look at the new notes in this book. What is your best suggestion for a new design for the $5 note?